This Will Remain With Us

Melissa R. Mendelson

Wild Ink Publishing

wild-ink-publishing.com

Wild Ink Publishing

A Wild Ink Publishing Original
Wild Ink Publishing
wild-ink-publishing.com

ISBN: (Paperback) 978-1-958531-10-5

You might not have been saving lives.

You might have just sat at a desk,
doing paperwork.

You may have stood next to a register, sliding
items across a conveyor belt.

Maybe, you were by yourself,
mopping the floor.

Still, You were on the frontline, and this book
*is dedicated to **All of You.***

Forward

I have had the privilege to narrate many of Melissa`s poems, and in doing so there is a degree of careful delivery that only comes with poetry written by a gifted hand. Melissa is indeed a writer, a poet, and a person, whose work is already stamped by her true visionary concepts. To have worked with her is always a creative joy, never needing to twist or bend a word, they are the words and the ink of a creative and talented lady.

—Alan Johnson

Table of Contents

When I Stepped Out Onto the Front lines

When I stepped out onto the front lines, I didn't know what I would see.
Everything seemed normal, the way it used to be.
The same everyday faces and the usual constant places.
The past was still leaving its traces.
All of it to be washed away.

Heroes on the Front Lines

I can't imagine what you see on the front lines.
All those cries for help.
All those lives begging to be saved.
You fight to save them,
but your hands are tied.
It's like performing open-heart surgery with one hand,
and they keep coming.
You keep fighting,
but the supply line is cut.
Help lies in the distance of an orange sky.
There are no copters in the air.
The enemy is unseen,
growing in number,
and laughing at failed attempts,
waiting for the front lines to break.
You stand strong,
determined to save as many lives as you can,
haunted by those lost
in the darkest of night,
but their pale faces don't incite fear.
They piss you off,
and that anger is fuel
to grab death by his throat
and say it's enough.
The war wages on.
The dust hasn't settled yet.
There will be so many dead,
but many more would be lost,
if you surrender the front lines.
I don't know what you see.
I can't imagine it,
but I do know
that you will fight.
You will fight until your last stand.

My Home's A Stranger to Me

I don't recognize my home.
It feels like a fortress.
We are locked inside,
staring out at an uncertain world.
When we venture out,
we count the moments until we're back,
safely behind these walls,
but are we a trojan horse?
Is time counting down until the attack?
Will we live?
Will we die?
I no longer recognize my home.
We're sitting in shadows,
holding to seconds passing
with night fading into day
and day burning into night.
The walls close in.
I can no longer look outside.

Thank You for the Dead

When this is over,
we are going to look for someone to blame.
We are going to point the finger and say,
"You lied to me.
We barely made it over the curve,
and you said that we would get through this."
When this is over,
there is no going back to normal.
Too many lives are destroyed
or will be destroyed.
Again, because you couldn't tell the damn truth,
and the news is not any better,
creating nightmares that find me at night.
I can't help but think of the movie, Watchmen,
the Comedian.
Is this all a joke to you?
We are supposed to be working together,
not passing the blame buck around and around.
When this is over,
the lives that could have been saved
will be lost,
and it will be because of you.
Thank you for the dead.
Don't talk about going back to normal.
Maybe, some might forget and forgive you
when this is over.
Others won't.
I never will.

Storm Over Hudson

I would rather seek refuge at home,
but I am out of time.
Those that could run
have already jumped ship,
but the other cogs in the machine
are forced to turn.
We're spinning like mad teacups,
trying not to lose our grip.
We are risking our lives to work,
seeking solace from those high above,
but we're being hung out to dry,
pawns to their Bishop.
If only I had the time,
but the doomsday clock will crack.
And it will crack.
No more time.
No haven to seek.
We are contamination.

The Life of a Grunt During the Coronavirus

The nights are the most quiet.
Unbearable and deadly.
The enemy could be lurking close,
but we still close our eyes.
We mutter a silent prayer under our breath
and thank the heavens when we wake up,
if we wake up.
We endure the long days.
Walk endless miles.
Far from safety
with a weapon that barely protects us.
The enemy could attack at any moment.
We'll never see it coming
because we're in their jungle now,
sinking deep into the mud.
The real heroes marched ahead,
diving courageously into war

while we trudge behind,
wondering why we're here.
We are no heroes.
We are not saving lives.
We should be home,
Safe,
away from danger,
but we are
Here,
on the front lines.
Stuck deep in the mud,
someone had lost their glove.
A soldier had fallen.
I saluted them
and trudged on.
A bullet missed my head.
Too many close calls,
but we can't go home.
We have to stay here.

Who is Protecting Me?

The weekends never felt so safe before.
The door locks behind me on Friday,
and I can breathe.
I don't have to go outside for two days.
Saturdays are great.
I rest, read, and write.
Sundays are about the same.
Sunday nights are different.
A dread starts to curl up inside my stomach.
Tomorrow through Friday, I have to go outside.
I have to go to work.
No lives rest in my hands,
but my life lies in theirs.
I do not have a choice.
Any moment, I could be exposed,
if not already.
I could bring the virus back,
and then, no one home will be safe.

Do You Think I Want to Be Here?

"Do you think I want to be here?"
He leaned close.
Hands pressed against the desk.
Words carved like a knife.
"My wife is sick."
"Not with Coronavirus,"
he quickly added.
"She can't go to a doctor.
Her medicine is on hold.
I should be home with her,
but I am here.
With you."
He waited for my answer.
Lips pressed tight.
Anger barely suppressed.
Tension coiled around like a noose.
I remained sitting in my chair.
His mouth opened,
but he was done,
storming away
back to his office.
Silence sliced apart by the door slamming shut.

They're Not Toy Soldiers Anymore

The grandmothers kissed their young farewell,
their hearts crying on the inside.
Their babies were going to war.
Despite the horrors happening,
they are first responders,
and they would risk their lives
to save more.
They are heroes,
even if it meant them dying,
but would their strokes of metal
deliver a deafening blow,
a defiant scream,
a gasping declaration
to call more to the fight,
if they did fall?
The grandmothers held hands,
cried their painful tears.
Their love gone into the fray.
Maybe tomorrow, they would return home,
but they would never be the same.

I Don't Want This Change

Everything has changed.
I did not want to accept that,
clutching onto normal,
refusing to let it go,
but normal has already gone.
Nothing is the same.
I don't know what is going to happen.
When this year began,
I actually made a plan.
There were a few monkey wrenches thrown in,
but I could deal with that.
I can't deal with this.
I can't deal with the fear waiting for me around the corner.
I can't deal with the hope that maybe this will end soon.
Things are unpredictable,
and everything is still changing.
And I worry.
I pray for normality to return,
but even when it does,
nothing will ever be the same again.

Striking Matches to See if We Burn

You might tell me that it is okay,
but this is far from over.
I'll take the assignment,
but I'm not dropping my guard.
The masks and gloves will still be used.
I'll Lysol spray my shoes
and jump in the shower when I get home.
I've crossed the line already,
and I don't know if I was, am, exposed.
Too many people in the post office without masks.
The girl standing close in the bagel shop.
Constant trips to the pharmacy and supermarket.
I'm playing a high-risk game,
and I don't need you to up the stakes.
But you tell me that it is okay.
What if you're wrong?
What if we are all wrong?
Then, there will be nothing left to say except,
"I am so sorry for your loss."
I hope to never hear you say those words.

I Miss Living Normal

I want things to go back to normal.
I'm tired of thinking of COVID-19.
The enormity of this virus is too much,
too much for my brain to bear.
Every thought traced with such fear.
I'm afraid the fear will never fade,
and my guard must remain up,
if not for myself,
then for those close to me.
I still think of normal.
Maybe, I'll see you again.

The Three Wise Men and Will McAvoy

I've stopped watching the news.
I can't take it anymore.
It's like a knife to the gut,
a bullet to the bone.
We all know the harsh reality that holds us.
We see it every day when we go outside.
A woman walking her dog while wearing a mask.
A couple wearing masks and gloves to go into the Post Office.
Yellow, ugly arrows pointing, "This Way" in a grocery store.
Kids sitting on their cars, talking as if life were normal,
then pulling up their shirts to cover their mouths as police drive by.
We don't need to watch the news to be terrified.
We need to watch the news to be informed,
and there is nothing wrong with a laugh or two.
We could always use a huge cotton swab to lighten the mood.
We can't be so serious all the time, or so worried.
We need wise men to tell us like it is,
but touch it up with humor.
Make us shake our heads.
I do not know about you,
but in my house
when the sun sets on another day
and another night comes to whisper of the same dread
waiting for me tomorrow,
that's when the wise men come in.
John Oliver, Bill Maher, and Chris Cuomo.
They make my family and I laugh.
They make us think.
They shed light over a darkness that's not going away any time soon.
They pass the nights
that fill in-between the days of constant dread,
and if he were a real man,
I would watch Will McAvoy from The Newsroom every day.

No Antibodies Found

I bit the bullet and took the antibody test.
I watched the nurse carry the vial of blood away.
There was no use worrying over it,
but I was sure that I would have antibodies.
I was sure that I was exposed to COVID.
I got the results today.
No antibodies were found.
Was I never exposed,
and if I was never exposed,
what do I do now?
Now, I have this sense of fear.
I don't want to go outside,
and I am allowed to work from home some days.
What do I do about the other days?
Do I let my fear take over?
Do I allow terror to run my life?
I don't want to be caged between four walls,
but I've seen people outside gathering,
not wearing any mask.
It's a no-win situation.
I need to live my life.

Maybe, It's Better You Are Not Here

I could be living a different life right now.
A life filled with more panic.
A life probably without my job.
A life in constant fear,
not knowing what lies in wait tomorrow.
I would count the passing days,
and I would pray every night.
I would go insane
because the child I almost didn't have
would be cradled in my arms,
looking at me to save them
when I can't even save myself.
Maybe, it is a good thing
I decided not to have a baby last year.

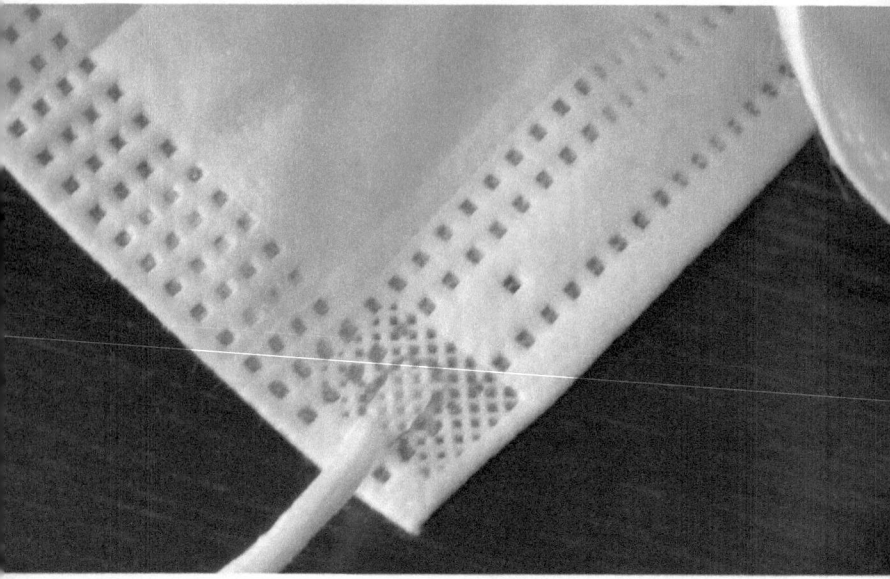

We Live in a War–Torn Pandemic Country

The conference room was cramped.
The air conditioner rattled behind me,
blowing out cold air.
The man behind me refused to wear his mask.
Only after a few jagged looks
and finally, a directed comment
did he raise his mask,
but I was the villain in the room.
Everyone stared at me,
blaming me for the disruption,
but it was mere distraction.
No one wanted to think of why we were here,
but our managers wanted to know
how did we feel about the whole COVID-19 situation.
And I could tell they were tired,
worn out from the frontline,
angered and upset at hands being tied,
no PPE to protect them or those in their care,

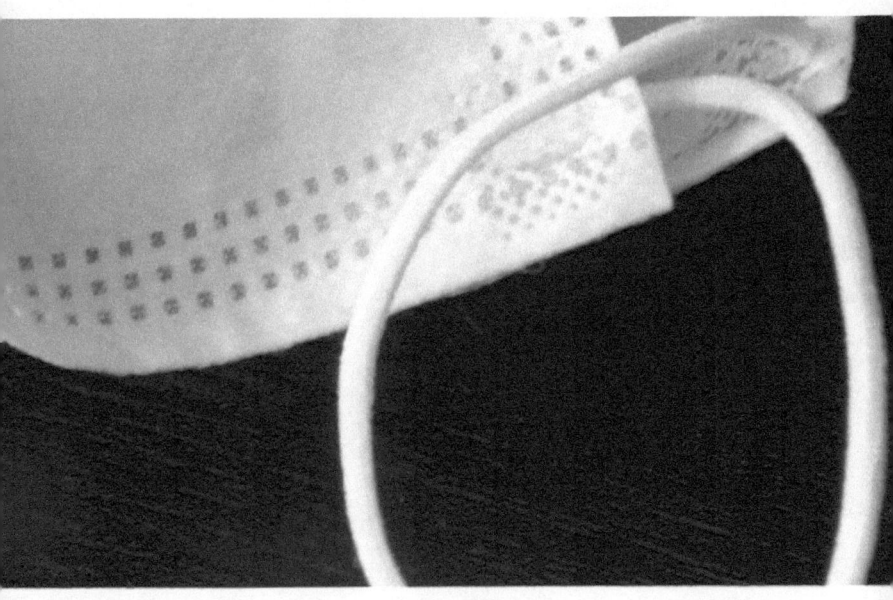

and knowing this pandemic was far from over.
Their fear drenched the walls.
Their thoughts hung in the air,
some comments razor sharp.
Faint hope was given
that their words would be heard and considered.
We will be ready next time.
I wanted to believe that,
but as they pushed their chairs slowly back
to leave the room
and step again on the frontline,
emptiness filled the room.

We Are All Dodging COVID Bullets

I feel like Neo from The Matrix,
dodging constant COVID bullets,
and I know a few brushed close,
maybe too close,
maybe some I didn't even know.
I'm on the defense,
armed to the teeth,
ready to dodge,
but the bullets keep flying.
And Agent Smith is still laughing,
making some people believe
the COVID bullets aren't real.

COVID's Got a Real Ugly Face
Just Ask Those Who Have Seen It

We're told that our enemy is invisible.
It has no face,
but only those that are on the frontline see it.
They see it every day,
masked in pain and anguish,
grinning because it thinks it won,
and it keeps on taking more lives away.
And our hearts are broken.
We say the names of those lost,
light a candle in their memory,
and when we close our eyes at night,
its face is waiting to be seen
because again, it thinks it won.
Maybe, it has,
and even if some can't see its face,
it will still be etched into our memory
when the day comes when it's gone,
if it's ever gone.
And more lives it will take,
hoping for us to surrender,
but those on the frontline
will keep fighting.
They will never give up.

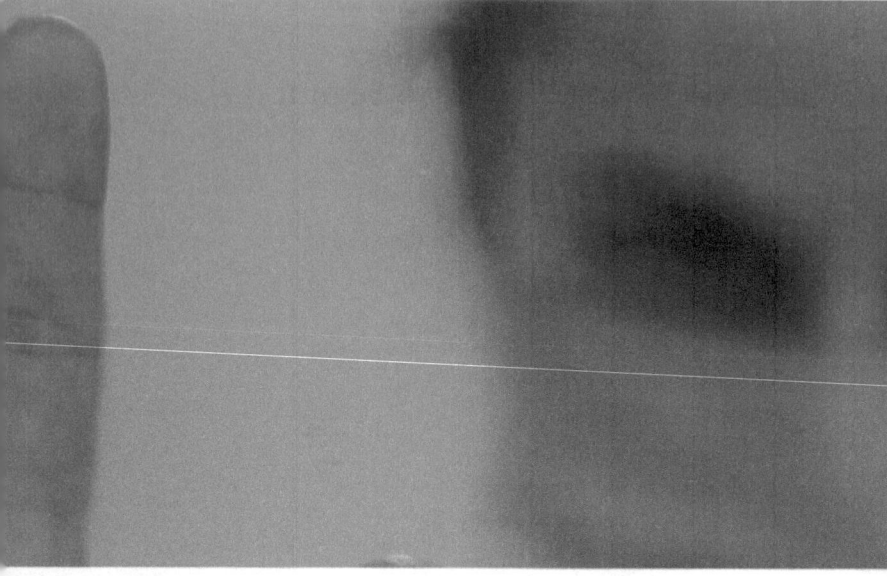

A Hero Stands Here

Inspired by The New York Times Presents: They Get Brave

The battlefield is quiet.
You've stood for so long,
seen so much loss of life.
You tried to give hope.
Some rallied against the system,
demanding to be seen,
to get help,
and sometimes Kelley, we need to be critical.
But we shouldn't have to pay the price,
if we, you are trying to save lives,
and so many came to you for help.
So many are still,
even if they don't believe in the virus,
but you've seen those rooms.
You've heard the ventilators,
the cries and prayers.
You felt the loss
as the war raged on,

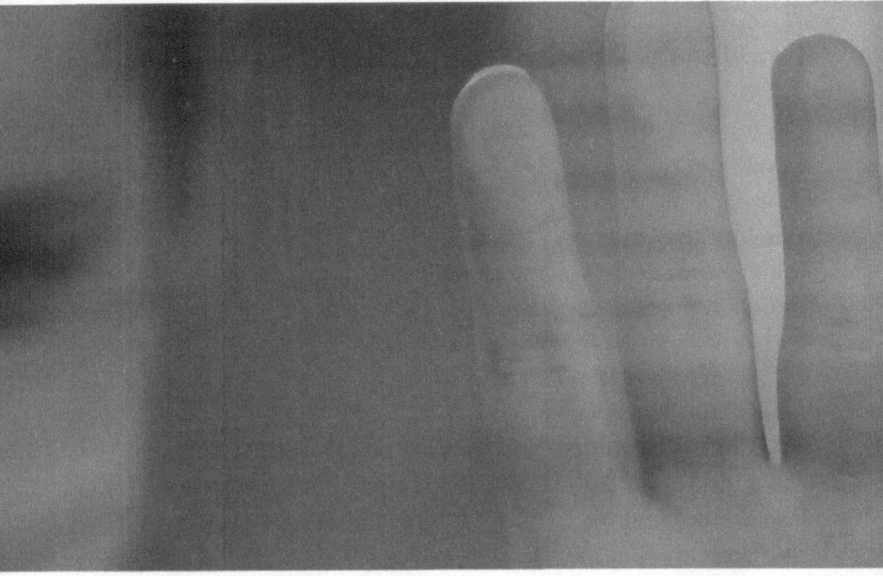

and even when the wave pulled back,
you knew that it would return.
And you're tired, worn down,
but you still stand.
And you wonder,
why are you not stronger?
But you are.
And you keep moving forward,
and yes,
"The losses far outnumber the victories.
Death is everywhere."
But you don't surrender.
You stay.
You fight.
You try to save lives.
If not for you,
we would lose hope,
and we need to remember that.
And we need to say,
"Thank You
for being the Hero that you are."

I'm Not Okay with You, Covid

I'm not okay with you, Covid.
I don't want you in my house
or visiting my friends.
I don't want you at my job,
touching my keyboard and phone,
riding on the backs of others
and looking at me over their shoulder.
I don't need you standing next to a guy
outside the bagel place,
smoking his cigarette before putting on his face mask
to go inside.
I don't need you.
You scare the shit out of me,
but you won't be ignored.
You'll be there.
You will always be there
until you are not,
and when you are gone,
you will not be missed.
I hope you leave soon,
and leave me be.

This Will Remain with Us

In the days to come,
we'll carry it in shadow.
Bury it in mind.
Whisper its name.
Flinch at yesterday.
My life is gone.
I'm not the same,
maybe not as damaged as others,
but I cannot look back anymore at yesterday.
What matters now is what happens today,
what will happen tomorrow,
and what kind of person I will become.
No matter the journey that lies ahead,
this will remain with us.

Here Lies a Name

I walked into the employee bathroom,
turning on the lights.
I sat down and waited to do my business.
As I waited, I stared out across the floor.
A name caught my attention.
It was carved across the tile.
My eyes traced over the name
and found another next to it.
And another, followed by yet another.
The floor was carved with employee names.
I recognized one.
They died of Covid.
Why carve their names into the floor
and not written on the walls?
Because it could be erased.
They would be forgotten.
I finished my business,
washed my hands
and stepped out of the bathroom.
But I didn't turn off the lights.
I returned a few minutes later
with a letter opener in my hand.

We Will Hold The Front Line

I listened to the sirens in the distance.
The danger knocking at my door.
I don't want to leave the safety of my home,
but I have to answer the call.
I have to hold the front line,
and I grabbed my gear,
gloves and a mask.
I glanced at a photograph of my family.
I was taking a risk,
a risk that could threaten them
and end everything that we know,
but they needed me.
I stepped up to the front line.
I do not call myself a hero,
but I know that there are heroes.
And I might not be saving lives,
but being out there is helping all those that are.
I press against the front line.
I hope with each and every day
that this nightmare will end.
I know that heroes will fall,
but we cannot fail them.

So, here I will stay,
staring down at the gaping viral abyss
with death looking back at me,
but I will not break.
I will fight,
and they will fight with me,
holding strong together,
never to surrender the front line.

This is How We Remember Them

The governor changed his mind about the memorial.
The spot was set but now left barren.
Nobody would know what was supposed to be there.
All this because someone had to complain.
I passed this spot every day, hoping to see a reminder
of those that put their lives on the line,
lost their lives
because they were trying to save us.
I couldn't walk by anymore.
I stood by the spot,
turned on the flashlight on the cell phone,
and raised the phone high into the air.
My hand folded over it,
and I thought of the nurse that held my hand
as my best friend struggled to breathe in the I.C.U.
I thought of her arm around my shoulders
as I cried my heart out
the last day that I went and tried to see him.

This Will Remain With Us

She didn't make it either,
and she looked tired
the last day that I saw her.
I won't forget her,
but she's just a memory now.
How long will that memory last?
There should be a memorial.
I lowered my hand,
but the light did not go out.
I looked behind me,
and my eyes met a gathering crowd.
The flashlights were switched on their cell phones.
Their hands were raised high into the air.
Tears streamed down their faces.
They knew someone,
lost someone,
and they remembered them.
The world needed to remember them too,
and I raised my phone up,
shining light
over that vacant spot.

I was heading toward Chester, New York when I saw these signs that children had made. A moment later, I turned the car around to look at them again.

Melissa R. Mendelson learned the art of poetry in her high school days when she struggled to find her voice and release the emotions that she kept inside. A lot of those emotions were turbulent, raw, and some of those poems could be found in her poetry collection, *Fragments of Yesterdays Past*. She also has another poetry collection called, *Tears of Sand*.